<MISSION 1>

BUILDING A BLOG

Are you ready to take the first step toward being a pro coder? We'll begin by setting up a basic website where you will be able to post text, images, music, games, and more. Right now, we need to build the base, and then we can expand to include whatever you can dream up. This very first, important mission will give you all the building blocks you'll need to get started. Even super-advanced websites can't skip this step. So you're exactly where you need to be!

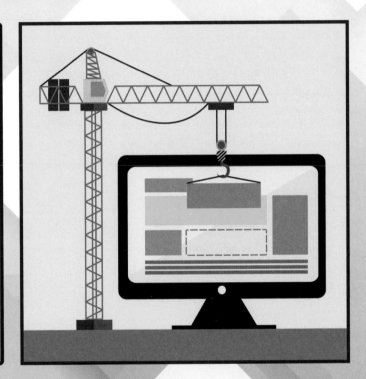

Ready, Get Set, Go!

1. Create a folder called **my site**. This folder is where we'll store all the pages we create and all of the images or sound files we want to use on the site.

Images and sound files are called website assets. Go ahead and make another folder called **assets** inside your **my site** folder.

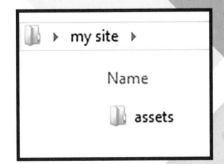

2. Open up your text editor program. Create a new document and save it as **index**, in the **my site** folder. You might notice a menu at the bottom that says **Save As Type**. If it gives you the option to save as **HTML** or **Hyper Text Markup Language**, choose this. Otherwise, just add **.html** to the end of your file name.

File name:	index
Save as type:	Hyper Text Markup Language file (*.html;*.htm;*.shtml;*.shtm;*.xhtml;*.xht;*.hta)

3. Now it's time to add some code! We'll be using HTML to build the basic parts of our blog. HTML uses **tags** to add things to a page. It's important to remember that most tags have to be closed, just like in the image below. If they aren't closed, things might look a little strange!

```
<head> <!-- Here, we open our tag -->
</head> <!-- Here, we close it -->
```

HTML always starts with the two lines to the right, so add them now:

```
<!DOCTYPE html>
<html>
```

See how we opened the **<html>** tag there? It now has to be closed. At the bottom of your page, type **</html>**. Great work!

Fun fact: Some tags can close themselves! For instance, the image tag looks like this: <img />

KIDS
CAN
CODE!

FUN WAYS TO LEARN
COMPUTER PROGRAMMING

BY IAN GARLAND

Sky Pony Press

Sky Pony Press books may be purchased in bulk at special discounts for sales promotion, corporate gifts, fund-raising, or educational purposes. Special editions can also be created to specifications. For details, contact the Special Sales Department, Sky Pony Press, 307 West 36th Street, 11th Floor, New York, NY 10018 or info@skyhorsepublishing.com.

Sky Pony® is a registered trademark of Skyhorse Publishing, Inc.®, a Delaware corporation.

Visit our website at www.skyponypress.com.

Authors, books, and more at SkyPonyPressBlog.com.

10 9 8 7 6 5 4 3 2 1

Interior art by Ian Garland
Cover design by Brian Peterson
Interior book design by Joshua Barnaby

Print ISBN: 978-1-5107-4005-1
E-Book ISBN: 978-1-5107-4003-7

Printed in China

<CONTENTS>

A NOTE TO PARENTS

We live in a world reliant on strong coders. These experts build the platforms required for our websites, our apps, and our electronics to work properly. And yet, despite the vast creative freedom that code offers, most tutorials focus on the boring parts: theory and memorization.

This book attempts to show children that coding can be more than a chore. It's a hobby that, if properly nurtured, can become extremely marketable (and profitable) in later life. Further, coding teaches analytical thinking while encouraging creativity. As with painting or sculpture, there really are no limits to what you can create, given enough time and practice.

The activities in *Kids Can Code!* will walk your child through basic coding principles step by step. We'll be covering design, animation, music, and gaming, so there's something for even the most hesitant learner. Hopefully, this book will mark your child's first step on a new and exciting journey of discovery.

Requirements

- A text editor

    For Windows users, Notepad is fine, as is Text Edit for macOS. That said, we recommend using the color-coded interfaces offered by the following programs, if possible.

    For Windows: Notepad++
    Available at: https://notepad-plus-plus.org

    For macOS: Atom
    Available at: https://atom.io

- A web browser and Internet connection. Certain aspects of HTML5 do not function properly in Internet Explorer or Mozilla Firefox, so using Google Chrome is recommended if at all possible. It's important to allow popups on the pages we create by clicking the button at the right-hand side of the address bar.

    Google Chrome is available at: https://www.google.com/chrome/

PART ONE

DIVING INTO DESIGN

4. We're almost done setting up our file. Just like you, an HTML file has a **<head>** and a **<body>**. The head is where we put important things that affect the entire page; it's easy to remember if you think of the <head> tags as the brain of your webpage.

The body is where we put everything that we want to show up when we load the page in a browser. It's like your site's T-shirt—the first thing a visitor will notice! Go ahead and add the <head> and <body> tags like so:

```
<!DOCTYPE html>
<html>

<head>
</head>

<body>
</body>

</html>
```

Playing with Tags

5. Okay, our HTML page is good to go! Now we can add some content, but first, you'll need to know about some of HTML's other tags.

Inside your **<body>** tags, enter the following code:

```
<p> Hi, welcome to my blog! </p>
```

The **<p>** tags let you enter text onto your site. They also add a new line underneath so that everything stays nice and neat. Why not save your file and double-click it to see what it looks like?

```
Hi, welcome to my blog!
```

TAG, YOU'RE IT!   X

HTML has loads of tags that let you change the way your text looks! What happens if you enter the following code snippets into your **<body>** section?

- <h1> Hello! </h1>
- <b> Howdy! </b>
- <u> Hi there! </u>
- <i> Hey! </i>
- <ul> <li>One </li> <li> Two </li> </ul>

6. We're going to add a set of **<div> tags**. But what is a div? Well, you can think of it as a divider—it helps keep different parts of your webpage separated. It doesn't actually show up on your web page, though—unless you add something inside them or change the way they look, **divs are invisible**.

Add the code below to your page, inside the **<body> tags**.

```
<div id = 'top'>

</div>
```

Whoa, we've added something extra in here! HTML lets you customize your tags by telling it a little more about them. Here, we've **given our div an ID** so we can change how it looks later. This ID can be whatever you like, as long as there are no spaces in it.

7. Now that we're getting the hang of HTML, let's add an image to our site. If you have a picture you think would work, great! If not, feel free to draw one using your favorite drawing program. Once you're done, give your file a name and **save it in the assets folder we made earlier**.

It's important to save it as a **.JPG** file. PNG files look better, but having too many can really slow your site down!

8. Back in our HTML file's <body> section, **add the following line**:

```
<img id = 'mainimage' src = 'assets/stickman.jpg' />
```

The **<img> tag** adds an image to a website. The **src** part gives the location of the picture we just drew. See, it's inside the **assets** folder. You should **replace stickman.jpg** with the name you gave your image, though! Notice how we also added an ID—this ID will be important later.

Go ahead and **put this image and your <p> tag inside the <div>** we created earlier!

9. **Save your file** and open it again in your browser. If everything's working, you should see your image on the website!

Believe it or not, you now know most of the HTML needed to create a great website! There is one small problem, though: black and white sites don't look all that impressive. In the next mission, we'll add some colors.

Hi, welcome to my blog!

<MISSION 2>

OVER THE RAINBOW: USING CSS

In this mission, we'll be using another important part of web design: Cascading Style Sheets, or CSS for short. These let us change the way certain parts of our website look. We can change their colors, move them around, and even flip them. Feeling artistic? Things are about to get colorful!

Creating Your CSS File

1. Open a new file in your text editor and save it as **style.CSS**. If there's a Cascading Style Sheets option in the **Save As** menu, great! If not, that isn't a problem. Make sure to save it in the same place as your **index.html** file.

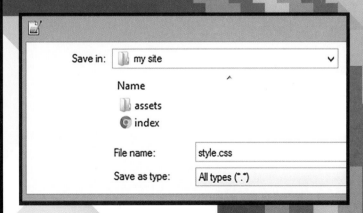

2. Now we have to tell our website where the CSS file is. We can do this with one line of code inside the **<head> tags**.

```
<link rel="stylesheet" type="text/css" href="style.css">
```

The important part here is the **href** section. This is where you type the name of your CSS file, which in this case is **style.css**.

Styling Your Page

3. Before we can get started, you have to understand how CSS works. There are three things to think about: the HTML tags you want to change, what you want to change about them, and what changes you actually want to make.

In the example on the right, we've selected the <p> tag and changed its color to red. Did you notice that the "p" isn't inside pointy brackets? In CSS, **we type the text inside the tags**, not the "<" and ">" symbols.

```
p {

    color: red;

}
```

Feel free to enter this into your CSS file. Save it, and your HTML page, then reload it. What happens?

Hi, welcome to my blog!

4. So what else can we change? How about the page's color? This is very simple. You can type the following:

```
body {

    background-color: blue;

}
```

Feel free to try entering different colors in here. Did you notice the problem? These colors are all a bit too bright!

5. To fix this color situation, we'll enter something called a **hex value** instead of using a color name. Hex values are strings of six numbers or letters with a "#" sign in front. They let you choose from a far greater range of colors, so let's find one that works.

Do a Google search for "CSS color picker." You can use the slider to adjust the colors and click until you find one you like. When you do, you'll see a hex code on the left-hand side. Type this into the **background-color** part of your CSS!

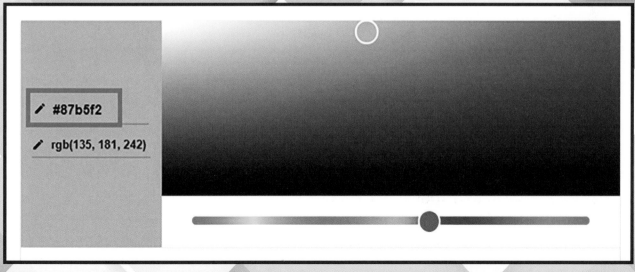

6. You can also use **hex values to change your <p> tags**. Find a color that works well with your background, and enter that into the CSS file instead of "red". For instance:

```
p {

        color: #f2f5f9;

}
```

7. Okay, now **save your CSS file** and reload the web page!

That looks a lot better, doesn't it? Okay, why don't we try a few tweaks to make the site look more modern?

Hi, welcome to my blog!

Cleaning Up

8. Enter the following code into your CSS file:

```css
#mainimage{

    float:left;
    max-width: 5%;

}
```

The "#" sign lets us apply CSS effects to an object with a specific ID. In this case, **our image's ID is mainimage**, so we typed "#mainimage". Get it?

We've told the image to hug the left-hand side of the screen, and we've also made it a little smaller. If you resize the page, you'll see that your image also changes size—so your website looks good when it's visited on a phone or tablet!

9. The text doesn't change size, though. Let's fix that! Inside your CSS file, type this:

```css
#top p{

font-size:  6vmin;
display:inline-block;
margin-top:2%;
margin-left:2%;

}
```

Take a look at the top part. We've told CSS to **change any <p> tags inside any element with the "top" ID.** The **font-size** part changes how big the text is. Try changing the number here and see what it does.

As for the **display** section, it tells the text to sit beside any other objects. We've added this part so that the text isn't above our image anymore. The **margin-left** and **margin-top** parts push the text just a little to the right and bottom of the page, so it looks more natural. What happens when you reload the page now?

Hi, welcome to my blog!

BE A CSS EXPLORER X

Here are a few more things to play with! Try entering these values into the image or text CSS. What do you think will happen? What actually happens? The first one only works with the image. Why do you think this is?

- border-radius: 25px;

- text-shadow: 2px 2px black;

- border-style: dotted;

- transform: rotate(180deg);

- opacity: 0.5;

- <ul> <li>One </li> <li> Two </li> </ul>

<MISSION 3>

JUMPING INTO JAVASCRIPT

So far, we've put some strong building blocks in place for a website. And that's a great start as we dive into more advanced coding and really wake up our page. Now it's time to reach for a tool called JavaScript. JavaScript lets us do all sorts of cool things, as you'll soon see!

Getting Set

1. Before we get started, let's add another section to the HTML page. This will allow us to keep all of our main content separate from our top section. **Type this in underneath your other <div> tags (not inside them)**:

```
<div id = 'main'>

</div>
```

Now in your CSS file, add this:

```
#main{

    min-height:50px;
    width:95%;
    background-color:white;
    border-radius: 25px;
    margin-left: 2.5%;
    margin-top:6%;

}
```

2. This coding gives us a white box with rounded corners in the middle of the page. Feel free to adjust these numbers if it doesn't look quite right to you—what's important is that it's **wide enough to hold lots of content**. Don't worry about the height since this <div> will grow as we put things into it. If you want to **add a margin-left value** to your image so it lines up nicely, now is the time.

Hi, welcome to my blog!

3. Go back to your HTML file. See where we've closed the <body> and <html> tags? After the **</body>** line, type **<script> </script>**. All of our JavaScript code has to go inside these tags.

Creating a Program

4. We'll start with something simple: a program that asks the user how old they are.

```
var age = window.prompt("How old are you?");
```

GETTING TO KNOW VARIABLES

JavaScript uses things called **variables** to store information for later. These variables can be numbers, words, or even lists of other variables. It sounds confusing, but it's actually fairly simple. Look at the image on the right:

```
var x = 5;

var y = 4;

var z = x+y;

var text = "Hello";
```

To create a variable, you type **var** followed by the variable's name. Then, you simply say what value you want to store. Easy, right? What value is stored inside the variable *z* in this example?

Now when you load the page, you'll be asked for your age. The number you type is stored as **a variable called *age***. But nothing happens afterward. Let's use **an IF statement** to change that! Type this code below:

```
if(age > 50){

    window.alert("Wow, you've been around for a while!");

}else{

    window.alert("Wow, that's really young!");

}
```

Do you understand how it works? If the *age* variable is more than 50, a popup appears displaying the top message. The **ELSE part** means that if the age is less than 50, users will see the second message instead.

4. There's a small issue, however. If you type a word instead of a number, you get the second message. We can fix this by putting the following code above the IF statement.

```
if(isNaN(age)){
    window.alert("That's not a number!");
}else{
```

We'll also have to add another curly bracket **"}"** to the end, underneath the second ELSE part. Now what happens if you enter a word instead of a number?

This code works by using one of JavaScript's built-in features called "*isNaN*". This is short for "is not a number," so in our example, we use it to see if the *age* variable Is Not a Number (isNaN). If it's not, we show a message. If it is, we continue on with the code we had at the start.

Are you getting the hang of JavaScript? Why not try the following challenges before moving on to the next mission:

- Make a message show up if the user says their age is 0.

- Make a message show up if the user says they're more than 120 years old.

- Create a message for users who are the same age as you.

- Try telling the user what number they entered. (Hint: put the variable outside of the speech marks and join it to the text with "+".)

COMPARING VARIABLES   X

Sometimes you'll want to compare one variable to another. In JavaScript, there are a few ways to do this, depending on what you want to do:

- $x > y$ This checks if the variable x is **higher** in value than variable y

- $x < y$ This checks if the variable x is **lower** in value than variable y

- $x == y$ This checks if the variable x is **equal** to variable y

- $x != y$ This checks if the variable x is **not** equal to variable y

- $x == 5$ && $y == 5$ This checks if **both x and y are equal** to 5

- $x == 5 || y == 5$ This checks if **either x or y is equal** to 5

GOING LOOPY

Sometimes you're going to want to run a piece of code multiple times—without needing to enter code multiple times. That's where loops come to the rescue! We'll be using two different kinds of loops in this mission: one called a FOR loop, and one called a WHILE loop. Ready to go loop to loop?

Fun with FOR Loops

1. Let's start with FOR loops. Take a look at the image below:

```
for(i = 0; i <5; i++){

        window.alert("Hi!");

}
```

There are four main parts to a FOR loop:

- The first is the **starting number** (in the example, this is 0).

- The second is the **ending number**. In this case, the loop runs as long as *i* is less than 5.

- Third, we have **the number to increase *i* by** each time the code runs. Here, we've written *i++*, which is just a short way of saying "add one to *i*". We could also have written "*i = i +1*".

- Since *i* starts with a value of 0 and ends when it reaches 4, this means it'll run five times in total.

- The fourth part is easy to remember: it's **the code you want to run** each loop!

2. We're going to need to add a button to our HTML page. **Put the following code inside your 'main' <div>:**

```
<button class= 'mainbutton' type='button' onclick = runFor()>Try a FOR loop</button><br>
```

Here, we've added a class to our button. **Classes are just like IDs**, but they're for **when you want to apply the same CSS effects to lots** of similar items. For instance, we want all of our buttons to look the same, so we give them a class instead of an ID. What's that <br> tag for? It just adds a new line to our HTML page!

The text between the <button> tags is what shows up on your button. **Try typing something different in here**. See how it changes?

3. Now we're going to **add a link to something called jQuery**. jQuery lets us do all kinds of neat things, but it also makes it easier to add new items to our page with JavaScript.

Because jQuery is quite a large file, it's easier to tell our site where to find it online, instead of downloading it for ourselves. In your HTML page's <head> section, **add the following line**:

```
<script src="https://ajax.googleapis.com/ajax/libs/jquery/3.3.1/jquery.min.js"></script>
```

WHAT EXACTLY IS JQUERY?   X

jQuery is a collection of JavaScript functions that we can use to control the items on our page. Let's look at some examples:

- **Deleting an element:** $('element-name').remove()

- **Creating a new element:** $('body').append("<p>Hello!</p>");

- **Make something happen when element is clicked:** $('element-name). click(function(){ })

- **Make an item fade away:** $('element-name').fadeOut();

4. We're going to use jQuery and a FOR loop to add pictures to our page. Go into your CSS file and **add this code**:

```css
.loopimage{

        position:inline-block;
        max-width:5%;
        margin-left:2%;


}
```

Remember how we used the "#" sign to tell CSS we wanted to target a specific ID? The "." sign just tells it to target a class instead.

5. Okay, **put the following code** into our <script> tags at the bottom of the HTML page:

```javascript
function runFor(){

    for(i = 0; i <5; i++){

        $('#main').append("<img class = 'loopimage' src = 'assets/stickman.jpg'/>");

    }

}
```

Here, we've created a function called *runFor*. **A function is a mini program that you can run whenever you like**. Notice how we added **onlick = runFor()** to the button we created? This runs our function whenever the button is clicked.

6. The line inside our loop adds a stickman image to our 'main' <div> every time the code runs. We can test this by **saving our pages and clicking the button** on our web page.

Try a FOR loop

And that's all there is to FOR loops! So what exactly is a WHILE loop?

Giving WHILE Loops a Whirl

7. With a FOR loop, you have to say how many times the code should run. What if you don't know how many times to run it? That's where we'd use a WHILE loop! **Enter this code** inside your <script> tags at the bottom of the page:

```javascript
function runWhile(){

    var age = window.prompt("How old are you?")

    while(isNaN(age)){

        age = window.prompt("How old are you?")

    }

    window.alert("That's a good age!");

}
```

We've created a **new function called *runWhile*** that asks the user for their age. Next, we check to see if the age is a number or not. If it isn't, we'll ask them again and again until they enter a number instead of text. Once they've done this, we display a message. Simple, right?

8. There's one last step: We need to **change our button's "onclick" value so that it runs the *runWhile* function instead of *runFor*.** When you're ready, save the page and try this new loop out!

From this page

How old are you?

OK   Cancel

Learning More About Loops

Are you beginning to understand how loops work? Once you're comfortable with them, try out these slightly more difficult tasks:

- Make your FOR loop run ten times instead of five.

- Comment out your age popup by putting "/*" at the start and "*/" at the end.

- Add an IF statement to your WHILE loop that displays different messages depending on the age entered.

- Make your FOR loop add text instead of an image.

- Add a message to the page every time an invalid age is entered. You might have to change your text color in the CSS file to make it show up!

FUN WITH FUNCTIONS

We've already created some simple functions, but in this mission, we'll be going deeper into how they work. You'll need just a few hints on how to make functions work best before we can get going with creating a more advanced function. With this knowledge, you'll be able to build all kinds of things!

The Golden Rules

1. There are two rules to think about when creating a new function. First, the name: **A function name should only be two words long, at most**. The first word is **usually a verb**, which is a "doing" word such as "get", "run", or "save". The second word is **almost always a noun** (naming word) such as "value", "number", or "details".

Remember: The two words have to be pushed together, and the first letter of the second word should be capitalized to make it easier to read! Can you spot which of these functions aren't named correctly?

- getValue
- myfunction

- storeName
- grabobject

- changeItem
- strongPassword

2. Ideally, **a function should have one specific job**. Maybe it's to get a value, add things to your page, or make something happen, but once that's done, you should create another function to do anything else. You don't need to have loads of one-line functions, but the smaller they are, the better.

This way makes it easy to find out which parts are causing problems and gives you greater control over when exactly a function runs.

3. Did you notice that we always put brackets after our function names? For instance, our button's "onclick" section says *"runWhile()"*. This is because you can use something called **parameters** to pass values into your function. It sounds complicated, but when you look at the code, it's actually fairly simple:

```
var x = 5;
var y = 4;

function addNumbers(number1,number2){

window.alert(number1+number2);

}

addNumbers(x,y)
```

In the example above, we tell the addNumbers function to use two parameters, *number1* and *number2*. It then adds these two numbers together and displays the answer in a popup.

We can pass whatever we want in now. The example shows us using two variables, but you could also run the function with *"addNumbers(5,4)"* or whatever numbers you like.

PUZZLING PARAMETERS   X

We've seen that a function can take parameters, but it might act differently based on what values you pass to it! What happens if you try running this code with the following parameters?

- Two different numbers
- "One" and "Two"
- *x-y* and *y-x*
- "1" and "2"
- *x*+3 and *y*+2

Go Far with Functions

4. Okay, let's try building a more complicated function. Type this into your script tags and change your button to run *"addImages()"* when clicked.

```
function addImages(){

    for(i=0; i < 10; i++){

    imageID = "image"+i;

        $('#main').append("<img class = 'loopimage' id = '"+imageID+"'src = 'assets/stickman.jpg'/>");
        rotateImage(imageID, i*20);

    }

}
```

First of all, we start a FOR loop that runs ten times. That's simple enough. Can you work out what the next part does?

It takes the word "image" and the current value of *i* and sticks them together to **create a unique ID for each image**. For example, our first image has the ID of "image0", the second has "image1", and so on.

Next, we add an image to the page, using our new ID. Notice the use of **both single (' ') and double (" ") quotation marks** here. If you need to use multiple sets of quotation marks, make sure the single marks are always inside the double ones, because otherwise your code might not work properly.

See how we added our *imageID* variable in here? It's outside of all the quotation marks and stuck to the text **using a plus sign (+)**. This can get confusing pretty quickly, but it helps if you think of this line as "FIRST PIECE OF TEXT"+*imageID*+"SECOND PIECE OF TEXT".

Our last line runs a function called *rotateImage* using the *imageID* variable and *i**20 parameters. This second value is how much we're going to rotate the images by each time. In JavaScript, the * symbol means to multiply, so it's the current value of *i* times 20. As *i* increases, so will the angle!

Value of *i*	Angle
0	0
1	20
2	40
3	60
4	80
5	100

5. Sounds cool, doesn't it? Well, first we need to **create the *rotateImage* function**. Below the function you just built, type this:

```
function rotateImage(imageID, angle){

    $('#'+imageID).css({transform: "rotate("+angle+"deg)"});

}
```

There's a lot going on here! Let's unpack it piece by piece.

The first parameter we pass to this function is called *imageID*. It passes a value such as "image0", "image1", or "image2" to the function. However, **jQuery needs us to put a "#" sign before an ID**, so we've stuck one to the front of our variable.

The next part is something new: you can actually apply CSS effects to specific things using jQuery. This is great for timing events: you want something to spin around when clicked, for instance.

The last part tells our site how much to rotate an image. Again, look how we've added our *angle* variable into it. The positioning of the quotation marks is very important!

6. **Save everything** and try clicking the button on your site. If everything has worked as intended, you should see ten overlapping, rotated images.

That's more like a flipbook than a real animation. This is how animation works, though: one image at a time. Luckily, there's a much easier way to move objects around our pages . . . which we'll explore very soon!

BLAST OFF WITH ANIMATION

MAKING SOME ASSETS

A lot of people don't realize how import-ant code is. Traffic lights, cell phones, and even rocket ships only work because of hard-working coders who make sure every-thing goes according to plan. Of course, it's not always hard work—you can code for fun, too! Why don't we start by making an ani-mation of a rocket blasting off and landing on the moon?

Let's Get Set

1. First, we have to **create the images** to animate. Open up your favorite drawing program and create a big circle. This circle is going to be planet Earth, so fill it with a sea blue color, then add some green splotches for land.

2. Next, color the background black. Space is dark, after all! Once you're done, drag your image to the top-left and use the handles at the side to cut away as much empty space as possible.

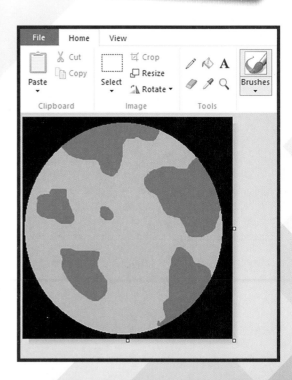

3. Finally, click the **Save button**. Name the file **"earth"**, and click the **Save as type** menu. Choose the **JPEG** file format. PNGs are higher quality, but if you have a lot of them, your website can take a long time to load.

File name:	earth
Save as type:	JPEG (*.jpg;*.jpeg;*.jpe;*.jfif)

4. Okay, now we'll draw a picture of the moon! This one's easy: it's just a large gray circle with some craters inside. Feel free to make your drawings as simple or as detailed as you like. Lots of people draw very basic pictures to start with, just to make sure the animation works, before going back and improving their drawings later.

Just like before, make the background black and trim away as much space as possible. Once you're done, save your image as **"moon.jpg"**.

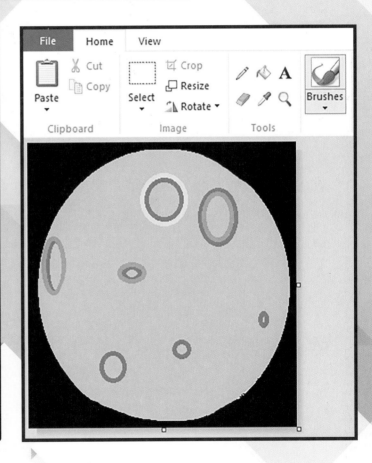

5. Our final drawing is going to be a rocket ship. You can draw whatever kind you like: a realistic ship, a futuristic shuttle, even an alien rocket. The great thing about coding (and animation) is that there's no limit to what you can do! Save your drawing as **"rocket.jpg"**.

Build the Base

6. Now that we've gathered all of our images (also called **assets**), we need to create somewhere to put them. We're going to build an **HTML page**, but don't worry, it's really simple when we take it step by step.

Open up a new file in your text editor program and save it as **"animation.html"**. Before we launch in, now is a perfect time to check out "HTML Hints" on page 39. Then, when you're ready, enter the following text into your HTML page:

```html
<!DOCTYPE html>
<html>

<head>

</head>

<body>

</body>

</html>
```

Remember, the **<head>** section is where we put important information that affects the entire page. The **body** is where we put the items we want to see. Simple, right?

HTML HINTS

Just like it's great to know some facts about a new friend, it's good to know these pointers when getting to know HTML.

- The first line should always be "<!DOCTYPE html>".

- The second line should always be "<html>".

- We use sets of tags to build HTML pages. Tags are just elements like <p> (paragraph), <div> (a container element), and <img> (an image).

- Most elements also need a set of closing tags with a slash before the first letter. For instance: <p> </p> or <div> </div>. There are some exceptions, though, such as the <img> element, which only needs one tag and can be closed like this : <img />.

7. Now, let's add our images:

```
<body>

    <img id = 'rocket' src = "assets/rocket.jpg"/>
    <img id = 'moon' src = "assets/moon.jpg"/>
    <img id = 'earth' src = "assets/earth.jpg"/>

</body>
```

You'll notice we've added an **ID for each image**. This lets us **target** them and change various things about them.

8. Targeting comes with the help of another **CSS file**. So add a link to this file in our <head> section now:

```
<link rel="stylesheet" type="text/css" href="style.css">
```

The problem is that we don't actually have a file called "style.css". This is okay, though: Just open a new file in your text editor and save it as **"animation-style. css"**. Make sure it's in the same folder as your HTML page!

9. It's time to see where we are. What does our website look like right now?

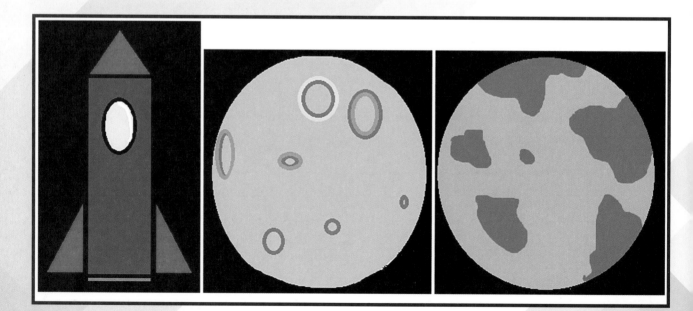

Okay, that's not perfect, but we're getting there. Why don't we arrange things with a bit of **CSS**?

10. In CSS, we target specific elements by typing their HTML tags, but without the pointy brackets. We can also **target individual IDs by entering a # sign before it**. For example:

```css
body {

        background-color:black;

}

#earth{

        float:left;
        margin-top:32%;
        width:20%;


}

#moon{

        float:right;
        width:15%;

}
```

See how we changed the <body> section, and also the Earth and moon images? Try saving your CSS file and reloading the web page. What happens?

That's good, but our rocket is bigger than the moon and just hanging in space!
Let's change that with some CSS:

```
#rocket{

    height:15%;
    position:absolute;
    margin-left:5%;
    margin-top:24%;
    -webkit-animation: blastoff 15s 1;
}
```

Your rocket should now be sitting near Earth! You might have to change the height and margin values a little, depending on how big your drawing was. Now, see that last line? That tells your rocket to use the "blastoff" animation. That doesn't exist *yet* . . . .

Code for Lift-Off!

11. Let's **create the code** needed to get this rocket to the moon!

```
@keyframes blastoff {

    10% {margin-top: 1%;}
    20% { transform: rotate(45deg); }
    60% { margin-left: 78%; margin-top:4%; }
    80% { transform: rotate(-90deg); }


}
```

These percentages tell the rocket when to do the actions in the brackets. Here, we make it rise to the top of the screen, rotate a little, then fly to the moon and rotate again. Because animations always return an element to how it was at the beginning, our rocket will fly right back to Earth when it's done!

12. It's been a great journey so far, but there's one last thing that'll really make this animation look amazing. Open up your drawing program, create a big black background, and draw some stars! When you're done, save this as **"space.jpg"**.

Now go back to the CSS file and add this under the body section:

```
background-image: url("space.jpg");
```

Save it, and refresh your web page. Wow, doesn't that look out of this world?!

<MISSION 2>

CUSTOMIZING YOUR CREATION

In Mission 1, we made all the basic parts of our rocket animation. With that smooth start, now it's time to really get creative! In this mission, we'll be making our scene look more realistic and adding some fun new effects.

Return to the Rocket

1. Hey, have you noticed that our rocket is way too big? What if we made it start really small, then get larger as it flies through space? That will make it look like it's getting closer to us!

Guess what? We already know how to do this—it's only one simple **tweak to the keyframe animation** we created in the last task! Add this line into the keyframe section of your **animation-style.css file:**

```
70% { height: 15%}
```

2. 15%? That's the same size as our rocket is right now! If we want to see any changes, we'll have to **make it smaller**. Because it's smaller, we'll also have to **adjust the margins** so it can land back on Earth.

```
#rocket{

    height:5%;
    position:absolute;
    margin-left:8%;
    margin-top:30%;
    -webkit-animation: blastoff 15s 1;

}
```

3. **Save your files** and reload the page. How does it look? If it's a little too far to the right, feel free to **adjust the margin-left** value. If it's floating in space when you load the page, you'll want to **tweak the margin-top** value instead! Once you're finished, you should have something that looks the following image:

4. At the moment, our rocket only flies once, but in real life, people go into space all the time. The good news is that there's a really easy way to **tell our animation to run multiple times**!

Remember when we set up the animation? In the **#rocket** part of our CSS, we used this line:

```
-webkit-animation: blastoff 15s 1;
```

See that number at the end? That's the number that says how many times to run the animation. At the moment, it's "1", but we can change that to whatever we like. If you want your rocket to fly back and forward forever, **replace the "1" with "infinite"**.

Launching Excitement

5. The most exciting part of a rocket flight is the launch, isn't it? Why don't we make this part more fun? To do this, we'll need to **add a couple of lines to our <head> section**. These tell our page where to find jQuery UI—a JavaScript package that lets us use some really cool animations.

```
<script src="https://ajax.googleapis.com/ajax/libs/jqueryui/1.12.1/jquery-ui.min.js"></script>
<link rel="stylesheet" href="https://ajax.googleapis.com/ajax/libs/jqueryui/1.12.1/themes/smoothness/jquery-ui.css">
```

6. Next, we have to **add another <div>** to our page. Put it **underneath your <img> tags**, and **give it the ID "smoke"**.

7. **Add the following code** to the bottom of your CSS file:

```
#smoke{

        position:absolute;
        height:50px;
        width:50px;
        background-color:grey;
        border-radius: 25px;
        margin-left: 7.5%;
        margin-top:32%;


}
```

When you reload your page, you should have a gray circle sitting roughly where your rocket lands.

Looks strange, doesn't it? Why don't we spice things up with some JavaScript?

8. Between the </body> and </html> tags, type **<script> </script>**. We're going to animate this little circle and make it explode!

9. **Enter the following** into your <script> tags:

```
$('#smoke').effect("explode", "slow" );
```

When you reload the page, you should see an explosion as the rocket blasts off!

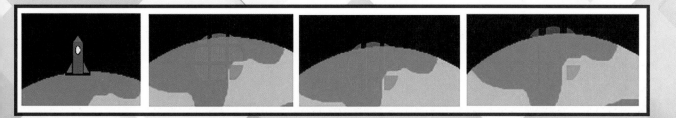

10. But wait—it only happens the first time! To make it happen every time, we have to add more code just below:

```
setInterval(function(){

    $('#smoke').effect("explode", "slow" );

 }, 15000);
```

What does this code do? Well, *setInterval* is sort of like the loops we covered earlier. It doesn't run a specific number of times, though. Instead, it **repeats the code inside the brackets based on a time**. See the number at the end? That means we want it to **repeat every 15,000 milliseconds** (that's 15 seconds). Why? Because that's how long our rocket takes to finish its animation!

Adding a Spin

11. Let's make one more change. In space, things are always spinning around. That's why the moon looks different every night! Can you think of a way to **make the moon rotate**?

Why don't we create another animation for it? In your CSS file, **add this**:

```
@keyframes rotate{

    100% {transform: rotate(360deg)}

}
```

12. Now we'll tell the moon to spin around. In the **#moon section**, add the following lines:

```
-webkit-animation: rotate 120s infinite;
animation-timing-function: linear;
position:relative;
z-index: 1;
```

This tells the moon to rotate really slowly for two minutes. The **z-index part** tells the moon what layer to be on. If we didn't have this, the black corners of the moon's picture might appear in front of our rocket ship!

13. Finally, add one more line to the **#rocket section**.

```
z-index: 2;
```

This is pretty simple: Our rocket has a higher number in the **z-index** part, so it appears in front.

BRINGING ANIMATION TO LIFE

Astronauts may not have found life in space yet, but that doesn't mean our animation has to be boring! In this mission, we'll be adding all sorts of cool things that will make your space scene really special.

Twinkle, Twinkle

1. Our starry background looks pretty good, doesn't it? Do you know what would make it better? If we could make some of the stars twinkle, like in real life! Luckily, with jQuery, we can.

The first thing to do is **create an array**. Arrays are **variables that hold several values** instead of one. The great thing about them is that you can grab specific values out of them whenever you like!

One thing to remember: **arrays start counting at zero**. This means the first thing in the array can be reached with "ARRAYNAME[0]". The second item would be "ARRAYNAME[1]", and so on.

```
var firstArray = [1,2,3];
var secondArray = ["You", "Can", "Store", "Words", "Too!"];
var thirdArray = [firstArray, secondArray];

var x = firstArray[0];
var y = secondArray[1];
```

What is the value of x in the picture above? And what about the value of y? Let's create an array with a few different colors in it, like so:

```
var colors = ["white", "yellow", "#f47a42", "#4e9eb2"]
```

2. Now we'll **create a function with a FOR loop** in it that runs 20 times. Can you remember how to do this?

```
function makeStars(){

    for(i=0;i<20;i++){



    }
}
```

3. It's time to really think about what we want this function to do. Let's say we want it to scatter stars across our scene and give them a random color. That sounds cool, doesn't it?

In this case, we have to do three things: we have to **randomly choose an X value** (how far to the right the stars go), **a Y value** (how far towards the bottom of the page they go), **and their color**.

This code looks really complicated, but it just grabs a random number for the star's X and Y values, before choosing a color from the array we created earlier. Type this into your function now:

```
starX    = Math.floor((Math.random()*90)+1);
starY    = Math.floor((Math.random()*50)+1);
starColor = colors[Math.floor(Math.random()*colors.length)]
```

4. Remember in our last mission when we gave **each image its own unique ID**? Well, we have to do the same thing here. Below the code you just wrote, add this:

```
starID = "star"+i;
$('body').append("<div class = 'star' id = '"+starID+"'></d
```

5. Okay, great! Now we have to actually **tell each star where to go and what color to have**:

```
$('#'+starID).css("margin-left", starX+"%");
$('#'+starID).css("margin-top", starY+"%");
$('#'+starID).css("background-color", starColor);
```

6. If you check your web page, you'll notice that no stars appear. Don't worry—there are two reasons why this happens. First, <div> tags usually don't show up if there's nothing inside them. Second, we haven't actually told our function to run yet!

We'll start by adding **a small piece of CSS so our stars appear**:

```css
.star{

    position:absolute;
    height:5px;
    width:5px;
    border-radius: 25px;


}
```

7. Now, we need to **add makeStars()** inside of our <script> tags, right at the top. If you refresh the website, you should see your stars appear. Better yet, refresh it again and you'll see that they've all moved!

8. These stars aren't twinkling just yet, though! For that, we'll have to add two more setInterval sections: one to fade the stars out, then another to fade them back in. Make sure to add this code **inside the <script> tags, but outside of your makeStars function**.

```
setInterval(function(){

    $( ".star" ).fadeOut( "slow");

 }, 2000);

setInterval(function(){

    $( ".star" ).fadeIn( "slow");

 }, 3000);
```

9. **Save everything and refresh** your page. You should notice that the stars we created now twinkle, just like the real thing! Great work!

LOOKING FOR AN EXTRATERRESTRIAL CHALLENGE? X

How well do you understand the code we've used? Once you have a handle, it's actually pretty easy to modify! If you're feeling confident, try out the challenges below:

- Create 50 stars instead of 20.

- Add a new color to the *color* array.

- Randomly change the size of stars.

- Make the Earth rotate like the moon. (Is there a problem with this?)

- Make the rocket take twice as long to complete its journey. (Hint: you'll have to change the CSS in the smoke's animation, too.)

<MISSION 4>

MAKING YOUR SCENE INTERACTIVE

Our out-of-this-world animation is really starting to look great! You know what would make it even better? If the user could make something happen. The changes we're going to make in this mission aren't all that realistic, but they're fun. And when you're coding, having fun is the most important part! Let's help our animation really take off step by step.

Creating Comets

1. As we get going, you should know one little piece of jQuery that lets you do a huge number of things: the **click function**. Here's an example:

```
$('body').click(function(){

    window.alert("Hi!");

})
```

With this code, a popup appears whenever the user clicks anything **inside the page's <body> tags**. Try it out for yourself—click the Earth, the moon, the stars, or the rocket!

Can you think of anything that pops up in space? What about comets? They appear and disappear pretty quickly, so they'd make a nice addition to our animation!

2. We'll start by creating a new **onlick function** at the bottom of our **<script> tags**:

```
$('body').click(function(){

})
```

3. We only want one comet onscreen at a time, so the first thing we do is **remove any others that are still flying around**. Then, we'll **create a new comet** to replace it. Type this inside your function:

```
$('.comet').remove();

$('body').append("<div class = 'comet'></div>");
```

Do you understand? We remove any item on the page that has the comet class, and then add a new one!

4. The problem with this is that all of our comets appear in the top-left of the screen. It might look like nothing happens, but that's because they're **empty <div> tags**. They don't show up unless we add something or tell them to appear in the CSS file, remember?

We'll get to that, but first, let's get these comets to appear in random positions. We can use some of the code we created earlier—the part that chooses a random position for the twinkling stars.

Underneath the last piece of code you entered, **add this**:

```
cometX  = Math.floor((Math.random()*90)+1);
cometY  = Math.floor((Math.random()*50)+1);

$('.comet').css("margin-left", cometX+"%");
$('.comet').css("margin-top", cometY+"%");
```

Flying in Style

5. Okay, it's time to **add some CSS**! We're going to tell our page that the comets should be small, round, and white.

```
.comet{

    position:absolute;
    height:5px;
    width:5px;
    background-color:white;
    border-radius: 25px;
    -webkit-animation: shootingstar 2s 1;


}
```

6. What's that last line? Another animation! It doesn't exist yet, so let's go ahead and **create it now.**

```
@keyframes shootingstar{

    100% { margin-left:-5%; margin-top:10%;}

}
```

7. See how we used a negative number here? This makes the comets fly straight off the screen! **Save everything, then reload** your web page. Now when you click the Earth, you shoot see a comet fly off to the left of the screen!

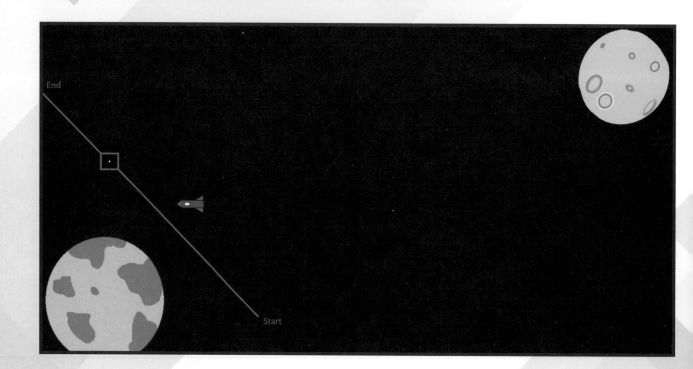

Your comets might not start in the same place, but they'll always fly to the same ending point. This is because we can't easily randomize CSS animations. Still, doesn't it look cool?

COMET CODING CHALLENGES   X

When you code, you're the boss. You can make whatever you like, and if there's something that you don't like, you can change it! The hard part is knowing what parts of your code to tweak in order to get the result you want. **For each of the tasks below, you'll only need to change one number in your CSS file**. Good luck!

- Make the comets move more slowly.

- Make the comets bigger.

- Change where the comets leave the screen.

- Make the comets squares instead of circles.

PART THREE

MUSICAL MADNESS

GETTING STARTED WITH SCRATCH

Why don't we switch things up a bit? There's a website called Scratch that lets you create programs by connecting blocks together instead of typing code. We're going to combine Scratch with what we learned in the previous coding mission to make some really cool music!

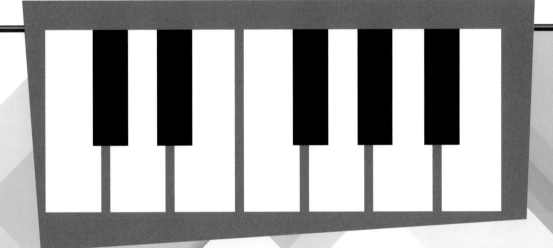

Setting the Stage

1. Open up your web browser and go to **https://scratch.mit.edu/**. In the top-left, you'll see a **Create button**. Click it, and you'll be taken to the page where we can start building!

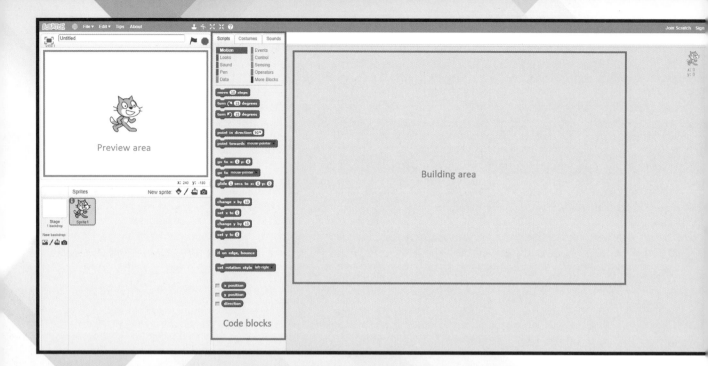

This page is split into three sections. On the left is the preview window, where you can watch your program take shape! On the right is the build area, where we'll be dragging blocks together to form programs. Right in the middle is the block selector, where we can choose the blocks we need.

2. Click on the **Events tab** at the top of the block selector section. You'll see a block that says **"When space key is pressed"**. Drag it over the building area now. Okay, let's make something happen!

Let's Play Piano!

3. We're going to add two new blocks here. Under the **Sound tab**, you'll find a **"Set instrument to 1"** block. Drag this out and connect it to the first one. Now do the same thing for the **"play note 60 for 0.5 beats"** block. What happens if you press the space key now?

4. Cool, we've created a very basic instrument! Of course, it's not much of a piano with only one note. Right-click on this code block and select **"Duplicate"**. See how we get another copy of the block? Do this until you have four of the same chunks of code.

5. At the moment, all of these blocks play the same note, on the same instrument, at the same time. The good news is that Scratch lets you change all of this stuff! See for yourself—try clicking the **"When space key is pressed"** block and **choosing a different button**. In the picture below, we've used the arrow keys, but you can use whichever you like.

```
when  up arrow ▼ key pressed
set instrument to 1▼
play note 60▼ for 0.5 beats

when  down arrow ▼ key pressed
set instrument to 1▼
play note 60▼ for 0.5 beats

when  left arrow ▼ key pressed
set instrument to 1▼
play note 60▼ for 0.5 beats

when  right arrow ▼ key pressed
set instrument to 1▼
play note 60▼ for 0.5 beats
```

6. Now it's time to change the notes that play. Click the **"Play note"** block and choose a new note for each. If you try pressing the buttons we assigned earlier, you'll realize that we've created an online piano!

```
when  up arrow ▼ key pressed
set instrument to 1▼
play note 60▼ for 0.5 beats

when  down arrow ▼ key pressed
set instrument to 1▼
play note 62▼ for 0.5 beats

when  left arrow ▼ key pressed
set instrument to 1▼
play note 64▼ for 0.5 beats

when  right arrow ▼ key pressed
set instrument to 1▼
play note 67▼ for 0.5 beats
```

Trading Instruments

7. What if we don't want a piano? Well, that's easy! Scratch lets you choose from 21 different instruments—click the **"Set instrument to 1"** block, and pick a new one from the list. Try this out. Which one is your favorite?

8. Think about your favorite song. It probably has a drumbeat, right? All the best songs do! Why don't we go ahead and add one to play along to?

This is nice and simple: drag out another "**When space key is pressed**" block. Now click **Control** and choose the **Forever block**. Remember the *setInterval* function? The Forever block works in exactly the same way!

9. Now we need to find our drum blocks. These are under **Sound**—just drag out two **"Play drum 1 for 0.25 beats blocks**." Finally, connect a **Rest for 0.25 beats block** and connect everything in order.

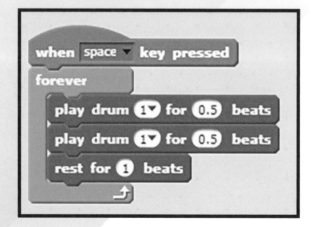

10. As you can see, we've changed the **speed of the drum** playing. One beat takes one second, so here, we've told our code to play two drumbeats per second. It sounds good so far, but by adding the code below, we can really take it to the next level!

We're all set up—try pressing the space key and playing along!

<MISSION 2>

ADDING BACKUP

Professional singers usually have backup singers—people who sing different but complementary notes during the song to make it sound better. Backup instruments can work in the same way. In this mission, we'll add backup music that you can play notes over the top of. Now, because our piano plays short notes, our backing melody should play long notes. If you want to play the backing music, it's easy—just flip it around and have the piano play long notes instead. Coding is so flexible!

Your Backup Block

1. Back in Scratch (https://scratch.mit.edu/), use what we've learned so far to **create this code block**:

```
when a ▾ key pressed
forever
    set instrument to 2▾
    play note 74▾ for 2 beats
    play note 76▾ for 2 beats
    play note 79▾ for 2 beats
```

Whoa, wait a second! The note selector only goes up to 72, so how did we get notes 74, 76, and 79 here? Well, if you double-click on the number, you can type anything you want. Careful, though—any notes over 100 are uncomfortable to hear and won't sound good in your song!

2. Once you're ready, start the drums by pressing **space**, and then kick off the melody by pressing the **A button**. Feel free to play the piano over the top!

Pumped-Up Piano

3. Hmm . . . Now that we've fleshed out the background music, our piano sounds a little weak. Why don't we code a few changes to make it a bit more exciting? We can do this by **making each button play a chord**. Chords are several notes played at the same time, and they're very easy to make in Scratch:

```
when up arrow ▾ key pressed
set instrument to 1▾
play note 60▾ for 0.5 beats
```

```
when up arrow ▾ key pressed
set instrument to 1▾
play note 64▾ for 0.5 beats
```

Notice how we didn't put the notes inside the same block? This is because they'd play one after the other, instead of at the same time! Try pressing the **left arrow** now. Doesn't that sound a lot better?

4. Go ahead and **do the same thing for all of your piano notes**. When you're done, you should have something that looks like this:

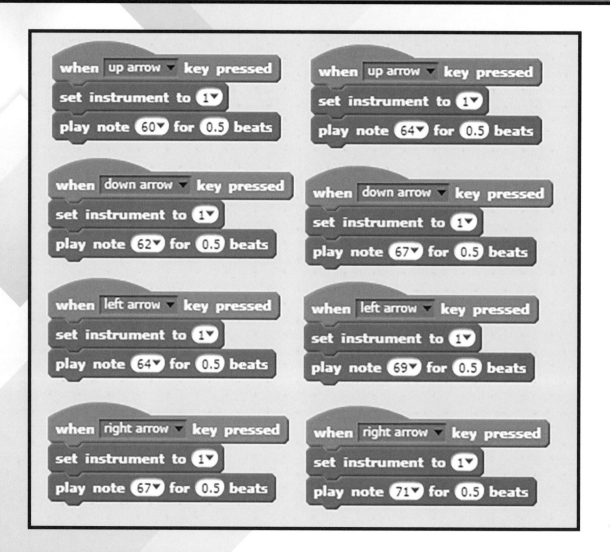

Rocking Out

5. It's time to really **have some fun**! Start the drums and melody, and try playing some music. If you feel like changing instruments, go right ahead! The synth (instrument 20) is a lot of fun and lets you make music that sounds like something out of a video game!

6. So far, our song is fun to play along with, but it really doesn't make you feel like you're a rock star. Why don't we change that? We can speed the entire song up by changing the tempo. Just add the **"Set tempo to 60 bpm" block** to the top of one of your drum loops, like so:

```
when  space ▼  key pressed
forever
    set tempo to  120  bpm
    play drum  1▼  for  0.5  beats
    play drum  1▼  for  0.5  beats
    rest for  1  beats
```

This block changes the speed of everything you play, not just the drums. It's 60 bpm (beats per minute) to start with, so what happens if we change this to 120? The drums get faster, and your piano notes really start to sound more like something you'd hear on the radio! Why not experiment with different values here?

<MISSION 3>

ADDING SOUNDS TO YOUR WEBSITE

Now that you've played around with sound blocks in Scratch, do you feel more prepared to actually code a music program? If not, don't worry—although the code might look pretty complicated, it's easier than it seems to set up music or other sounds on your website!

Assets First

1. We have some drawing to do! Open up your drawing program and sketch out a music note. Why not make the background your favorite color? Once you're done, save the file in your **assets folder** as **note.jpg**.

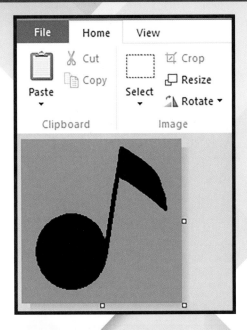

2. Okay, now create a new HTML page called **music.html**. We can copy most of the content straight from our **index. html** page, so you don't have to type everything out by hand.

```
<!DOCTYPE html>
<html>

<head>

    <link rel="stylesheet" type="text/css" href="style.css">

</head>

<body>

    <div id = 'top'>

        <p> Hi, welcome to my blog! </p>

    </div>

    <div id = 'main'>

    </div>

</body>

<script>
</script>

</html>
```

3. Let's **add five music note images** inside the main <div>:

```
<div id = 'main'>

    <img id = 'note1' src = 'assets/note.jpg' />
    <img id = 'note2' src = 'assets/note.jpg' />
    <img id = 'note3' src = 'assets/note.jpg' />
    <img id = 'note4' src = 'assets/note.jpg' />
    <img id = 'note5' src = 'assets/note.jpg' />

</div>
```

4. How does our page look? A little plain, right? **Let's write some CSS** to add a splash of color:

```
#note2{

    filter:hue-rotate(180deg);

}
```

So how does this work? Well, have you ever seen a color wheel like the one on the right? Basically, the code above **allows you to rotate it by a certain number of degrees**. For instance, our background was a light green, so when we rotate it 180°, it became a pinkish color.

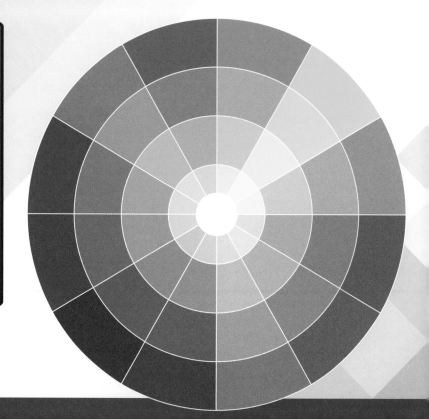

5. **Add CSS for the remaining note images now**. Try changing the numbers to see what kind of colors you can get! Here's a quick example:

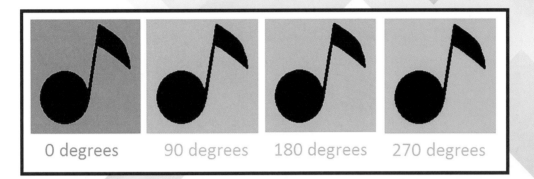

0 degrees   90 degrees   180 degrees   270 degrees

6. Our boxes are looking great, but they're still a little off-center. **Add this snippet** to your CSS file, and the problem should be resolved.

```
#note1{

    margin-left:25%;
}
```

Play That Music

7. Okay, now that we've sorted our assets out, we can get to the fun part: coding up some tunes! If you have a song or audio file on your computer, you can **make it play by adding this to your <body> tags:**

```
<audio src="music.mp3" autoplay>
</audio>
```

Of course, you'll have **to remember to change "music.mp3" to the name of your file**. That's not all—you can add a play/pause button by replacing the "autoplay" part with "controls".

<MISSION 4>

CREATING YOUR OWN INSTRUMENT

We made some good music in Scratch, but we could only choose from a limited selection of notes and instruments. In this mission, we'll use something called the Web Audio API to code up our very own instrument. Get ready to code, play, and take a bow!

Setting Up Sound

1. Before we can get started, we have to tell our page that we want to use the Web Audio API. To do this, **type the following code into your <head> section**:

```
<script>
    var context = new AudioContext()
</script>
```

2. Now, down in the **<script> tags**, we're going to **create and run a new function**. Don't be scared off by the first five lines of this function—those just set up the audio player the way we want it.

```
playNote()

function playNote(){

    var o = context.createOscillator()
    var  g = context.createGain()
    o.connect(g)
    g.connect(context.destination)

    o.start(0);

    var X=5;
    g.gain.exponentialRampToValueAtTime(0.00001, context.currentTime + X)

}
```

Save your page and try reloading it. What happens? You should hear a noise that sounds like a chime or doorbell. Great! Problem is, we only have one note.

3. We can add more notes by **allowing the *playNote* function to take a parameter**. Can you think of which lines we'd have to change to do this? Don't worry if you can't—check out the highlighted changes in the image below.

```
playNote(280)

function playNote(frequency){

    var o = context.createOscillator()
    var  g = context.createGain()
    o.connect(g)
    g.connect(context.destination)

    o.frequency.value = frequency;

    o.start(0);

    var X=5;
    g.gain.exponentialRampToValueAtTime(0.00001, context.currentTime + X)

}
```

4. Now when you reload the page, you should hear a different sound. Try passing in different numbers instead of 280. What do you think will happen? The rules are actually pretty simple: lower values make low sounds, and higher values make really high-pitched sounds!

Instrument Design

5. Okay, it's time to create our instrument! We're going to add an **onclick event** to our images to make them play a note whenever they're clicked. This is really easy; just **change your image code** to look like this:

```
<img id = 'note1' onclick=playNote(130) src = 'assets/note.jpg' />
<img id = 'note2' onclick=playNote(146) src = 'assets/note.jpg' />
<img id = 'note3' onclick=playNote(164) src = 'assets/note.jpg' />
<img id = 'note4' onclick=playNote(174) src = 'assets/note.jpg' />
<img id = 'note5' onclick=playNote(195) src = 'assets/note.jpg' />
```

6. **Try clicking on each of your images**. See how they each sound different? That's because each image runs the function with a different value. So how did I choose these values? That's easy—they sound good! If you try changing these values, you'll see how difficult it is to find five sounds that go well together.

A Little Tuning

7. We could call it a day right now, but coders are adventurous people! Plus, there are a few more things we can play around with in the Web Audio API.

At the bottom of our function, there are a couple of interesting lines of code.

```
var X=5;

g.gain.exponentialRampToValueAtTime(0.0001, context.currentTime + X)
```

The variable *X* tells our notes **how long they should play for**. What happens if you change *X* to 2? What about 15? You should hear a pretty obvious difference!

8. The other interesting part is the **number inside the final line**. This number tells our notes how quickly they should **fade out**. Because the value is so small at the moment, they fade very quickly. If we make this number slightly larger, say 0.0200, then the notes will ring out for quite a bit longer.

9. The Web Audio API even lets us change the way the notes sound. All we have to do is put this line in **underneath the "o.frequency.value"** part:

```
o.type = 'sine';
```

10. There are **four different effects** built in:

- sine: The default setting. This is the effect you've already heard.

- square: A slightly more electronic-sounding note.

- sawtooth: A very video-game style note.

- triangle: A soft, piano-style note.

Try changing the effect for yourself. Which is your favorite? What kind of music do you think it would be best suited to?

11. Finally, let's **add the ability to play chords**. There are two ways of doing this: we could either pass a second parameter in when we run the function, or we could do something to the first parameter to make a new sound.

The second way is simpler, so that's the one we'll use. If you think you can do it the first way, though, go for it! We've already covered everything you'll need to know earlier in the book, so feel free to look our previous missions if you get stuck.

To make our images play a second sound, we just have to **copy and paste our code**. Usually, we could use a loop of some kind, but the Web Audio API can be a bit temperamental sometimes, and it doesn't work very well with loops. Change your *playNote* function so that it looks like this:

```
function playNote(frequency){

    var o = context.createOscillator()
    var  g = context.createGain()
    o.connect(g)
    g.connect(context.destination)
    o.type = 'sawtooth';

    var o2 = context.createOscillator()
    var  g2 = context.createGain()
    o2.connect(g2)
    g2.connect(context.destination)
    o2.type = 'sawtooth';

    o.start(0);
    o2.start(0);

    o.frequency.value = frequency;
    o2.frequency.value = frequency*2;

    var X=5;
    g2.gain.exponentialRampToValueAtTime(0.00001, context.currentTime + X)
    g.gain.exponentialRampToValueAtTime(0.00001, context.currentTime + X)

}
```

That's a big function! However, we haven't actually changed very much. Can you see that we've made copies of the *o* and *g* variables? They're named *o2* and *g2*. We've also multiplied the parameter by two so that both notes aren't the same.

12. **Save your page and click an image**. Can you hear both notes playing at the same time? Excellent work! Can you come up with a song that would sound good? If you're really feeling adventurous, try using a different effect on the second note.

GET YOUR GAME ON!

<MISSION 1>

AMAZING MAZES

Many future programmers fall in love with coding when they try to figure out how games work—and how to code their own. While coding complex games can get pretty complicated, there is always a way to start out easy and still have fun. Games you know and love may have started with a really simple idea and basic coding before taking off in more adventurous directions. Here's a classic way to learn gaming through code: programming a maze!

Start with a Sprite

1. Open your browser and go to **https://scratch.mit.edu**. Click the **Create** button at the top, and we'll get started.

2. You'll see a cat in the **preview window** on the left. This is called a **sprite.** Sprites are what we call pictures that we'll be using in our game. Unfortunately, we're not going to be using him this time, so click the **paintbrush icon** in the toolbar.

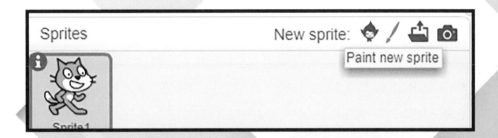

3. You'll see that a drawing panel has opened up on the right. Go ahead and use the tools to **draw a square**. When you're done, color it in. Then try to place it right in the middle of the drawing area.

4. Now, right-click the cat and select **Delete**. You could also click the **scissors icon** at the top of the page, and then click the cat.

5. Our square is way too big! Let's use the **shrink tool** at the top of the screen to cut it down to size. Click this icon, then click the square until it's nice and small.

Set Up Rules

6. Now we need to **add logic** to our game. What does that mean? Game logic simply tells the game what to do and when to do it. Why don't we start off by allowing our square to move around the page?

Drag out a **when space key is pressed** block from the **Events** tab. Next, connect a **point in direction 90** and **move 10 steps** block. Both of these can be found in the **Motion** tab. Finally, make this code run when the **right arrow is pressed** by selecting the right arrow inside the first block.

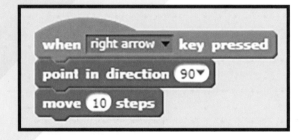

7. Right-click this code block and select **Duplicate**. Do this four times—one for each arrow key. We want our **up arrow to point in direction 0**, our **left arrow to point at -90**, and our **down arrow to point at 180**. That lets us turn the square around and move in the right direction.

when [right arrow ▾] key pressed
point in direction (90▾)
move (10) steps

when [left arrow ▾] key pressed
point in direction (-90▾)
move (10) steps

when [up arrow ▾] key pressed
point in direction (0▾)
move (10) steps

when [down arrow ▾] key pressed
point in direction (180▾)
move (10) steps

Try pressing the arrow keys now. Does your block move around like it should?

8. Can you guess the next problem? It's not much of a maze without any walls! Click the **paintbrush icon** again and **create two new sprites:** one rectangle lying on its side, and one standing upright. When you're done, you should have something like this:

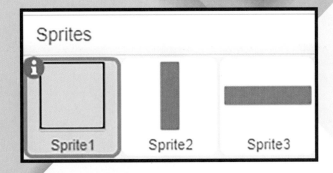

Sprites

Sprite1   Sprite2   Sprite3

9. Now, we're getting to the fun part! We're going to use these new sprites to **make some walls**. Right-click them and choose **Duplicate** if you need to, and try to use the **shrink** and **grow tools** in the top bar to make your walls larger or smaller. I've added an example below, but you can make your maze as simple or as difficult as you like. Just make sure it's big enough for the square to move through.

Our walls are gray, but yours don't have to be. The important thing is to make sure that every wall is the same color. I'll explain why very soon!

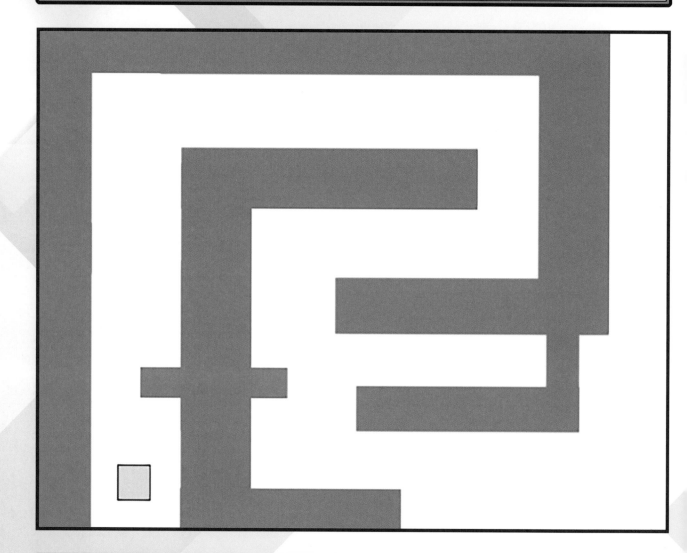

10. Try moving your sprite around. Notice anything strange? It can walk right through the walls of the maze, which obviously isn't very fair! Luckily, we can prevent this by **adding a little bit of code to each of our movement blocks**:

```
when [right arrow ▼] key pressed
point in direction (90▼)
move (10) steps
if < touching color [ ] ? > then
    go to x: (-150) y: (-150)
```

```
when [left arrow ▼] key pressed
point in direction (-90▼)
move (10) steps
if < touching color [ ] ? > then
    go to x: (-150) y: (-150)
```

```
when [up arrow ▼] key pressed
point in direction (0▼)
move (10) steps
if < touching color [ ] ? > then
    go to x: (-150) y: (-150)
```

```
when [down arrow ▼] key pressed
point in direction (180▼)
move (10) steps
if < touching color [ ] ? > then
    go to x: (-150) y: (-150)
```

First, grab an **IF/THEN** block from the **Control tab**. Next, add a **Touching color** block from the **Sensing tab**. Click the green square, then click one of your walls. Finally, add a **Go to** block from the **Motion tab**. The numbers here will move the square to the bottom-left when it touches a wall. Depending on the layout of your maze, you might have to change these numbers slightly.

A VALUE EXPERIMENT   X

Scratch does things slightly differently from HTML. In Scratch, a **value of zero for x and y puts you right in the center of the screen**. That's why we've used negative numbers here in Step 10. Why not play around with the values and see what happens?

Go for the Goal

11. So far, we have a working maze. The problem is that there's no reason to go through it! Why don't we **create a new sprite** and use that as a goal? **Draw a picture of a house** and place it at the end of the maze!

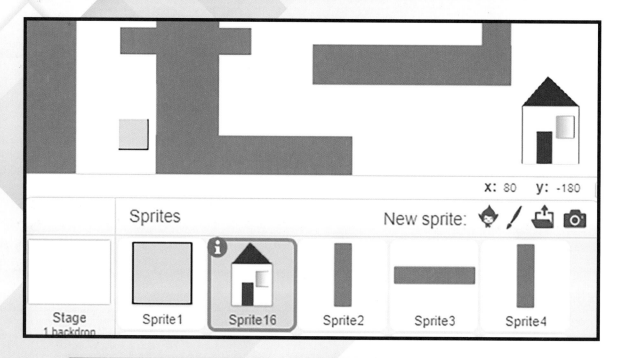

12. We're almost done! Next, we're going to **add a message** that pops up when you reach the house. We'll also have to **make sure that the square sprite disappears**—after all, there's no need to move around once you've won the game!

```
when right arrow ▼ key pressed
point in direction 90▼
move 10 steps
if     touching color ☐ ? > then
    go to x: -150 y: -150

if     touching Sprite16 ▼ ? > then
    say You win! for 2 secs
    hide
```

Now, in the maze we've created, it's only possible to reach the house by pressing the right arrow. However, if your maze looks different, you might have to add this last section to all of your arrow keys. Okay, let's see if that does the trick . . .

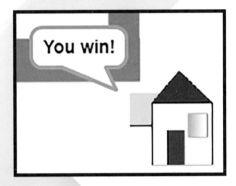

13. Excellent work! Okay, the square disappears after two seconds, but what if we want to play lots of times? We only have to **add one last code block** to make this happen:

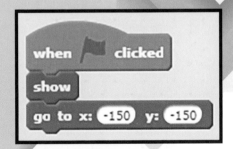

Now when you click the **green flag icon**, your game will completely reset. This lets you play as many times as you like!

FUN ON THE FARM

Now that you're good friends with coding basics for games—assets, logic, movement, and goals—we can try something beyond a maze. Let's put what we've learned into action and start coding a more eventful game, though it will take a few separate missions to bring it all together! The idea is simple: Farmer John is having a really bad day and needs your help. Mission 2 will get you well on your way with assets, a game base, and movement.

Assets First

1. Ready to create some game assets? Open up your drawing program and **draw a farmer**. It's important that he's a rectangle shape with no background, like in the picture below. When you're done, save it as **farmer.jpg.**

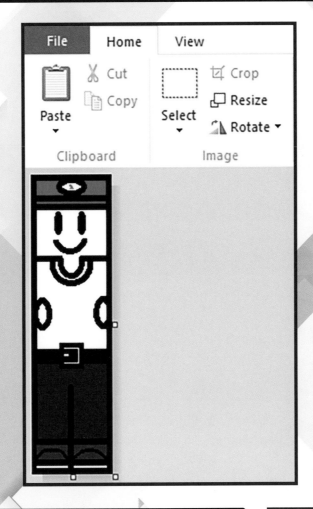

2. Now let's create an obstacle for our farmer to overcome. **Draw a picture of a pig** and save it as **pig. jpg**. You might have to use a few different shapes here, but if you take your time, you can make a pig that looks fantastic!

3. But won't that white background look weird when we use it on our website? Luckily, there's an easy way to get rid of it without coloring it all in. Open your browser and **go to https://www199.lunapic.com/editor/?action=transparent.**

4. You'll see a button that says **Choose file**. Click it, find **pig.jpg**, and hit the **Open button**.

5. You'll see your pig appear onscreen. **Click the white part.** The site will remove the background for you, leaving you with one good-looking sprite!

Finally, click the **Save** option at the bottom to download the file. Notice how it's a PNG file now? That's because JPG images can't have parts that are see-through. Once the image has downloaded, rename it **pig.png**.

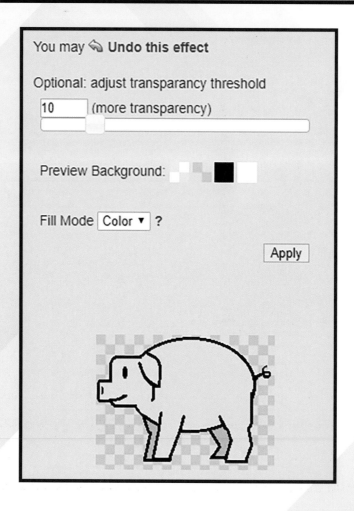

6. We have one more image to make! This time, it's going to be our game's background. When you think of a farm, what do you see? Probably a lot of grass, right? Take your time and **make a grassy background image** like the one below:

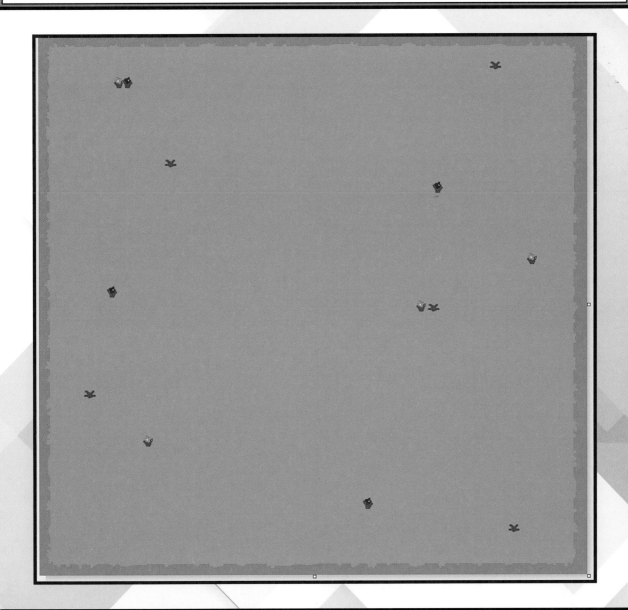

Once your field is looking good, save it as **field.jpg**.

Build the Page

7. Now it's time to **set up our web page**! Open up your text editor and type the following code in:

```html
<!DOCTYPE html>
<html>

<head>
    <link rel="stylesheet" type="text/css" href="game-style.css">
    <script src="https://ajax.googleapis.com/ajax/libs/jquery/3.3.1/jquery.min.js"></script>

    <script src="https://ajax.googleapis.com/ajax/libs/jqueryui/1.12.1/jquery-ui.min.js"></script>
    <link rel="stylesheet" href="https://ajax.googleapis.com/ajax/libs/jqueryui/1.12.1/themes/smoothness/jquery-ui.css">
</head>

<body>

    <button class= 'startbutton' type='button'>Start game</button><br>
    <div id = 'gamearea'></div>

</body>

<script>
</script>

</html>
```

Nothing new here—it's just a simple web page with a single <div> and a button to start our game.

8. Our page is trying to link to a CSS file called **game-style.css.** Only problem is, this doesn't exist yet. Let's create it now and add a little flair to the page!

```css
body {

        background-image: url("assets/field.jpg");
        height: 100%;
        overflow: hidden


}
```

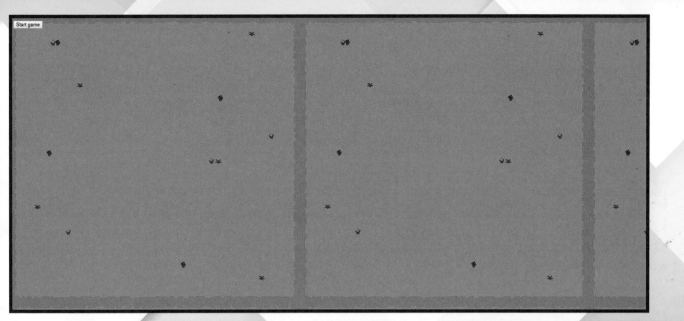

Start game

See how our background image is repeated? That's because our page is larger than the image. Normally, we'd have to fix this, but it actually makes our farm look more realistic, so we'll leave it as is for now.

9. So, when we click the **Start game button**, we want our farmer to appear. That's easy enough! Inside your <script> tags, add this:

```
function startGame(){

    score = 0;
    $('#gamearea').append("<img id = 'farmer' src = 'assets/farmer.jpg' />");

}
```

We'll also have to add **"onclick = startGame()"** to our button's code. Okay, save everything and try clicking the button!

Make a Move

10. Now it's time to make our farmer move around! He's a busy guy, after all, and he has a lot of work to do! Enter this underneath your **startGame function**.

```javascript
document.onkeydown = movement;

function movement(e){

    e = e || window.event;

    if (e.keyCode == '38') {
        console.log("up")
    }
    else if (e.keyCode == '40') {
        console.log("down")
    }
    else if (e.keyCode == '37') {
        console.log("left")
    }
    else if (e.keyCode == '39') {
        console.log("right")
    }
}
```

This code is tough to understand, isn't it? Basically, it waits until you press one of the arrow keys and displays a message in the log. You can check the log by pressing the **F12 key and clicking Console**.

So what are the numbers for? Well, JavaScript doesn't actually know what an arrow key is! Instead, it gives every key on your keyboard a number. Here, we can see that the up arrow is **key 38**, down is **key 40**, left is **key 37**, and right is **key 39**.

11. All that's left is to change the code inside this IF statement so that the farmer moves. First, go into your CSS file and give the **#farmer** a **margin-left** and **margin-top** value of 2%.

Now, when a button is pressed, we need to find out how far from the top and left of the screen the farmer is. To move him down the page, we increase the **margin-top value**, and to move him up, we decrease it, like so:

```
if (e.keyCode == '38') {
    up = parseFloat($('#farmer').css('marginTop'));
    $("#farmer").css("margin-top", (up-20)+"px");
}

else if (e.keyCode == '40') {
    down = parseFloat($('#farmer').css('marginTop'));
    $("#farmer").css("margin-top", (down+20)+"px");
}
```

Don't worry about the *parseFloat* function—that just removes things like "%" symbols or "px" from the CSS values so we're only dealing with numbers.

12. The code is almost exactly the same to move him to the right or left, only this time we change the value of **margin-left** instead:

```
else if (e.keyCode == '37') {
   left = parseFloat($('#farmer').css('marginLeft'));
      $("#farmer").css("margin-left", (left-20)+"px");
}


else if (e.keyCode == '39') {
   right = parseFloat($('#farmer').css('marginLeft'));
      $("#farmer").css("margin-left", (right+20)+"px");
}
```

Once you save everything, you'll notice that you can use the arrow keys to move the farmer around! Doesn't he look happy?

13. There is one small issue: if the farmer goes off the side of the screen, we lose him! We can prevent this by **adding a bit of code to each of our IF/ELSEs.** This code is starting to get pretty complicated, so I've highlighted the parts to change:

```
if (e.keyCode == '38') {
    up = parseFloat($('#farmer').css('marginTop'));

    if(up>0){
        $("#farmer").css("margin-top", (up-20)+"px");
    }
}

else if (e.keyCode == '40') {
    down = parseFloat($('#farmer').css('marginTop'));

    if(down<680){
        $("#farmer").css("margin-top", (down+20)+"px");
    }
}

else if (e.keyCode == '37') {
    left = parseFloat($('#farmer').css('marginLeft'));

    if(left>0){
        $("#farmer").css("margin-left", (left-20)+"px");
    }
}

else if (e.keyCode == '39') {
    right = parseFloat($('#farmer').css('marginLeft'));
```

Now, the numbers inside the IF statement check to see if the farmer is off the side of the screen and stops him going any farther. You might have to change the values if it doesn't work properly, though—just tweak them until they work on your screen.

Now, assure Farmer John you've got everything under control and can give him even more help in Mission 3!

WHO LET THE PIGS OUT?

Farmer John can now run around his field, so let's give him a workout. His pigs have escaped their pen and are running wild! The problem is that they're really big, really fast, and really strong, so John has to try his best to get out of their way. What can we do to take the next steps to program everything we need for this game?

Make Pigs Fly

1. Take a look at the code below. You'll recognize the *setInterval* function, right? It means that this code will **run every three seconds**. Then we choose which side of the screen the pigs will appear from using *Math.random*. Add this code **at the bottom of your <script> tags**.

```
function createPig(){
    setInterval(function(){

        $('#pig').remove()
        var direction = Math.floor(Math.random() * 2);
        $('body').append("<img id = 'pig' src = 'assets/pig.png'/>")

        if(direction == 1){

        }else{

        }

    }, 3000);

}
```

2. Okay, why don't we fill this IF statement out a little? Remember how earlier, I said it's tricky to randomly animate things on a page? Well, I think you're ready for the challenge!

```
if(direction == 1){

    $("#pig").css("margin-left", "-15%");
    $("#pig").css("transform" , "scaleX(-1)");
    $("#pig").animate({ 'marginLeft': '101%'}, 2000);
```

The first two lines are simple enough: We **start off with the pig off the left side of the screen**. Next, we **flip it** so he's running in the right direction. The last part is interesting: it works like a keyframe animation but lets us use variables! **Notice how there's no dash in "marginLeft"**—this is because the *animate* function works differently from most of the others.

3. So we know what happens if the direction equals one. What about if it's zero? That's easy!

```
}else{

    $("#pig").css("margin-left", "101%");
    $("#pig").animate({ 'marginLeft': '-15%'}, 2000);

}
```

In this case, we start the pig off the right side of the page and run him across to the left! **Inside your *startGame* function, type createPig();**. If you **save everything and click the Start game button**, you should see pigs running around!

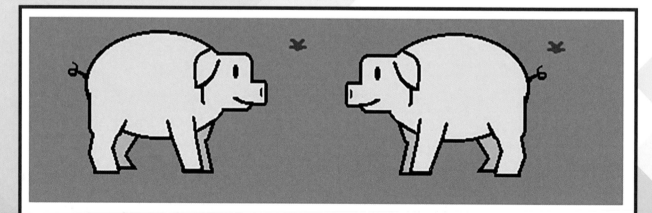

direction == 1   direction == 0

4. There is a slight issue. These pigs always appear right at the top of the page. Can you think of a way to fix this? Here's a clue: It **involves our good friends *Math. random* and jQuery's *CSS* function**:

```
pigY  = Math.floor((Math.random()*45)+1);

$('body').append("<img id = 'pig' src = 'assets/pig.png'/>")
$("#pig").css("margin-top", pigY+"%");
```

Add the highlighted lines to the top of your *setInterval* function. That's all it takes to let your pigs roam around!

Code the Collisions

5. You've probably noticed that nothing happens when the pig hits the farmer. Unfortunately, jQuery doesn't have a built-in way to tell if elements are colliding, so we'll have to use some math. First, though, let's **create a new function at the bottom of the <script> tags**.

```
function getContact(){

    setInterval(function(){

    }, 10);

}
```

It has another *setInterval* inside, and with a number so low, it's going to run all the time. Otherwise, your function would only recognize some of the collisions. Nobody wants to get hit by a pig, so it's important we know every single time it happens!

6. Remember how we used *parseInt* to grab CSS values for a specific element? We need to grab the **height, width, margin-left, and margin-top values** for the farmer and pig every time this code runs. Inside the *setInterval* function, type this:

```
var farmerX = parseFloat($('#farmer').css('marginLeft'));
var farmerY = parseFloat($('#farmer').css('marginTop'));
var farmerHeight = parseFloat($('#farmer').css('height'));
var farmerWidth = parseFloat($('#farmer').css('width'));

var pigX = parseFloat($('#pig').css('marginLeft'));
var pigY = parseFloat($('#pig').css('marginTop'));
var pigHeight = parseFloat($('#pig').css('height'));
var pigWidth = parseFloat($('#pig').css('width'));
```

7. There's a problem here, and it's because of the way web pages position elements. Let's say your farmer image is 100 pixels wide. **The entire image only has one X value and one Y value**—in its top-left corner. By **creating a few new variables**, we can tell the page to consider the entire height and width of the image:

```
var rightBuffer = farmerX+farmerWidth;
var leftBuffer = farmerX-farmerWidth;
var downBuffer = farmerY+farmerHeight;
```

8. Now that we have those values, we need to tell our page what to do with them. This next part is pretty complicated, but basically it tells the page to **create a popup** if the pig and farmer images overlap:

```
if (pigX > leftBuffer && pigX < rightBuffer && (pigY+pigHeight) > farmerY && pigY < downBuffer){

    window.alert("Hit!");

}
```

9. Finally, add **getContact();** to your *startGame* function. You can now save everything and start the game. You'll see the word "Hit!" whenever the pig touches the farmer.

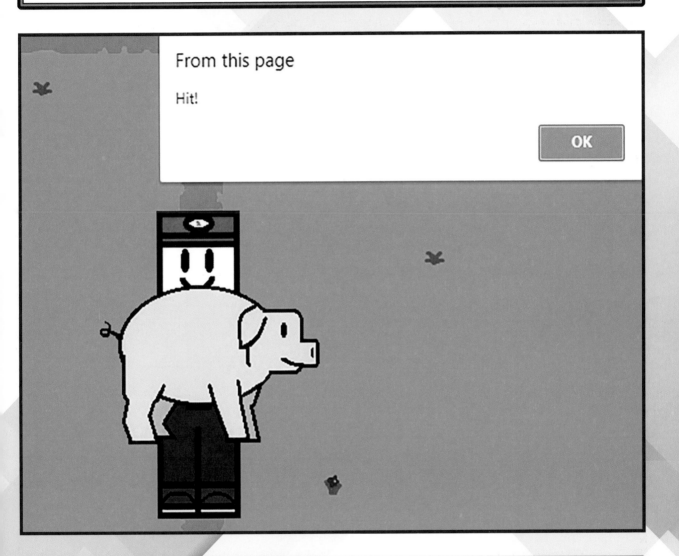

10. Having a popup while you're trying to concentrate on a game could be annoying. Why don't we give the player a way to tell if he's been hit?

The trouble is that the pig actually hits the farmer lots of times, since the images overlap for quite a while. This means we have to find a way to only apply an effect once. Right above your *getContact* function, add **var hit = 0;**

11. Now **replace your IF statement** with this, taking care to add the part at the end of the first line:

```
if (pigX > leftBuffer && pigX < rightBuffer && (pigY+pigHeight) > farmerY && pigY < downBuffer && hit == 0){

    $('#farmer').effect("shake", 100 );
    hit = 1;

    setTimeout(function(){

    hit = 0;

    }, 1000);

}
```

From now on, you should see the farmer quickly shake from side to side if a pig runs into him! We've stopped the animation from playing over and over by making it play once, and then waiting a second. This gives the pig plenty of time to run past you, stopping it from happening again. Neat, right?

Speed Play

11. Our game looks good and works well, but it isn't exactly fair. For example, the pigs move a lot faster than the farmer, and he's a pretty big target to hit. Why don't we give him a helping hand and even the playing field a little? There are two ways to do this: you can either make the farmer faster or the pigs slower.

To speed up the farmer:

Look inside your *movement* function. Inside your IF statement, there are four lines that deal with movement. They look like this:

```
if(up>0){
    $("#farmer").css("margin-top", (up-20)+"px");
}
```

Just make the value in the box higher to move faster, or lower to move slower!

To slow down the pigs:

Changing the pigs' speed is really easy—just change the value in the *setInterval* functions!

```
if(direction == 1){

        $("#pig").css("margin-left", "-15%");
        $("#pig").css("transform" , "scaleX(-1)");
        $("#pig").animate({ 'marginLeft': '101%'}, 2000);

}else{

        $("#pig").css("margin-left", "101%");
        $("#pig").animate({ 'marginLeft': '-15%'}, 2000);

}

}, 3000);
```

The number at the top changes the speed if they come from the left, and the second number changes their speed if they come from the right. The number at the bottom tells your page how often to create a new pig—**make sure this is higher than the numbers above,** or your pigs will disappear before reaching the edge of the screen!

MORE FARM EXCITEMENT   X

This section has been the hardest one so far. But if you're feeling up to the task, I have a few extra challenges for you until our next mission, in which we add a goal and scoring!

- Change the farmer's height.

- Make the pigs from the right slower than those from the left.

- Let pigs move diagonally. (Hint: Use "marginTop" in the *animate* section.)

- Make pigs change size randomly.

ADDING A GOAL

Farmer John and our pigs are getting a little tired. Our game goes on forever, and there's really no specific goal. Every programmer hits a point where they're not satisfied and need to push the code further, to do more. Why don't we advance our game now with more coding? Let's add a timer and a high-score system so that our players have something to aim for!

It's Time for a Timer!

1. First of all, we have to change our HTML page slightly. We'll **add three new <span> tags** to hold all of our game information. <span> tags are just like <p> tags, but they don't include a new line afterward.

```
<button id= 'startbutton' class = 'gameinfo' type='button' onclick =startGame() >Start game</button>
<span id = 'timer' class = 'gameinfo'></span>
<span id = 'scoreboard' class = 'gameinfo'></span>
<span id = 'highscore' class = 'gameinfo'></span><br>
<div id = 'gamearea' class = 'gameinfo'></div>
```

```css
.gameinfo{

    position:inline;
    color:white;
    margin-left: 2%;
    font-size: 2.5vmin;
    font-weight: bold;

}

#startbutton{

    margin: 10px;
    color:black;

}
```

2. Did you notice that all of these elements have the **gaminfo class**? Why don't we add a little CSS to spruce it up a bit? We'll also make the button a little bigger:

3. We have our timer <div> all set up. Now let's **create a function** so we can get our counter actually running! At the top of your <script> tags, type this:

```javascript
var score = 0;
var highscore = 0;
var gameLength = 60;
```

At the bottom of your <script> tags, type this:

```javascript
function timer(){

gameLength = 60;
document.getElementById("startbutton").disabled = true;

    var round = setInterval(function() {

    },1000)

}
```

The first thing this does is **create a new variable called *gameLength***. We'll be using this to change how long the game runs for. Next, we make it so that you **can't click the start button more than once** per game.

Lastly, we set up a new *setInterval* function that **runs every second**. What's the difference between this one and the *setIntervals* from earlier? It's stored as a variable—I'll explain why later.

4. Next, we need to check if the game is still running. That's easy—just see if the *gameLength* variable is **greater than zero**. If we take one from its value away every time the loop runs, we'll get ourselves a countdown!

Note that you have to add **timer()** to your ***startGame()* function.**

```
var round = setInterval(function() {

    if(gameLength > 0){

        gameLength = gameLength - 1;

    }else{

    }
```

5. Our *gameLength* variable now changes every second, but we can't actually see any difference just yet. Go ahead and **add the current value** into our timer <div>. We can also change the score and high score <div> while we're at it:

```
if(gameLength > 0){

    gameLength = gameLength - 1;

    document.getElementById("timer").innerHTML = gameLength+" seconds left";
    document.getElementById("scoreboard").innerHTML = "Your score: "+score ;
    document.getElementById("highscore").innerHTML = "High score: "+highscore ;
```

6. Finally, we have to decide what we want to do when the game ends. Let's count the tasks:

1. Remove the farmer.

2. Make the start button clickable again.

3. Stop the timer.

4. Stop pigs from appearing.

We can do the first three of these things by adding the following code to the **ELSE part** of our timer function:

```
$('#farmer').remove()
document.getElementById("startbutton").disabled = false;
clearInterval(round);
```

Remember how we stored our *setInterval* in a variable? By using *clearInterval*, we can stop the code from running!

7. Now let's stop pigs from appearing after the game ends. To do this, we just wrap most of the *createPig* code in an IF statement, like so:

```
function createPig(){

    var creation = setInterval(function(){

        $('#pig').remove()

        if(gameEnd){
            clearInterval(creation)
        }
```

8. So far, so good—our timer works perfectly!

Start game   57 seconds left   Your score: 0   High score: 0

The problem is that we don't actually have any way to increase the player's score yet. Can you think of any ways we could do this?

Setting Up Scoring

9. Let's say that if you **dodge a pig, you get ten points**. Careful, though—if it **bumps into you, you lose twenty points**! First, add **score = 0** to the top of your *startGame* function. This will reset the score every time you play.

10. Now go into your *getContact* function and **add the highlighted line** so that your IF statement looks like this:

```
if (pigX > leftBuffer && pigX < rightBuffer && (pigY+pigHeight) > farmerY && pigY < downBuffer && hit == 0){

    $('#farmer').effect("shake", 100 );
    hit = 1;

    setTimeout(function(){

    hit = 0;
    score = score-20;

    }, 1000);

}
```

11. Lastly, add the highlighted block of code to the **bottom of the *setInterval* inside your *createPig* function**:

```
score = score+10;

if(score > highscore){

    highscore = score;

}

}else{

    clearInterval(creation)

}
```

12. Now save everything and try your game out. If it's set up correctly, you should see your score go **up when a pig appears**, and **down if it hits you**.

Make sure that your high score increases, too! Wait for one game to finish and start a new one. Your **score should reset to zero**, but your **high score should stay the same**.

Start game   57 seconds left   Your score: 0   High score: 70

TASKS FOR BONUS POINTS   X

Was this task too easy for you? Try your hand at some of these:

- Make it so that you lose 100 points if a pig bumps into you.

- Make a game last 30 seconds instead of a minute.

- Change the color of your gameinfo text.

- Take ten seconds off the timer whenever a pig hits you. (Hint: you'll have to change where you set the *gameLength* variable.)

<MISSION 5>

MAKING THE GAME MORE FUN

How is the situation on the farm? Pigs don't appear all that often, and Farmer John has a lot of time to wander around. Why don't we add more challenge? First, we can add bonus goals to increase a player's score. What could that look like? As if farmer John wasn't having a bad enough day, the pigs keep stealing his lunch. So we'll help him get those sandwiches back as they appear in random positions!

More (Delicious!) Assets

1. The first thing we need to do is **draw a great big sandwich**. You can make it as crazy as you like, but **there's one rule to follow**: it has to be a square or a rectangle with no empty space. What do you think of my sandwich?

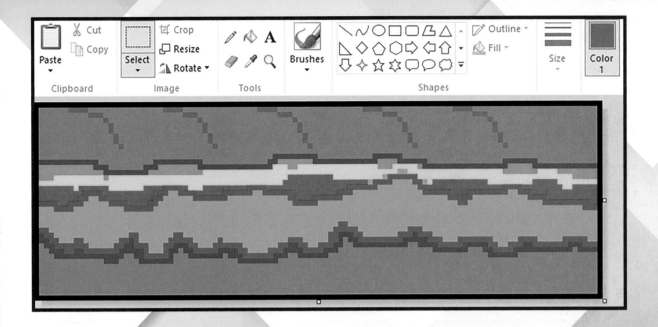

When you're done, save it in the **assets folder** as **sandwich.jpg**.

Moving Sandwiches

2. Okay, great! Just like the pigs, our sandwiches need their own function. Let's **create a really basic one** that checks to see if the game is over, and if not, runs our code every two seconds.

```javascript
function createSandwich(){

    var sandwiches = setInterval(function() {

        $('#sandwich').remove();

        if(gameLength>0){

        }else{

            clearInterval(sandwiches)

        }

    },2000)

}
```

3. If we want each of our sandwiches to appear in a random place, we have to pick a **random X and Y value**, just like we did with the stars back in the animation chapter. To do this, we'll add the following code to the IF statement:

```
sandwichX  = Math.floor((Math.random()*90)+1);
sandwichY  = Math.floor((Math.random()*50)+1);
```

4. We still haven't told the page to **make a sandwich appear**. Do that now, and tell it to use the random position we just created:

```
$('body').append("<img id = 'sandwich' src = 'assets/sandwich.jpg'/>");

$('#sandwich').css("margin-left", sandwichX+"%");
$('#sandwich').css("margin-top", sandwichY+"%");
```

5. Now, **add createSandwich()** to the bottom of your *startGame* function. We'll also add a little bit of CSS so that the pigs don't push the sandwiches out of the way:

```
#sandwich{

    position:absolute;

}

#pig{

    position:absolute;
}
```

It All Adds Up!

6. If you start a new game, you should see that sandwiches pop up regularly. We're almost done! However, nothing happens when you catch a sandwich. To change that, we'll need to create one last function. The good news is that it's very similar to our *getContact* function.

Enter this at the **bottom of your <script> tags**:

```javascript
function sandwichContact(){

    var detectContact = setInterval(function(){

        var farmerX = parseFloat($('#farmer').css('marginLeft'));
        var farmerY = parseFloat($('#farmer').css('marginTop'));
        var farmerHeight = parseFloat($('#farmer').css('height'));
        var farmerWidth = parseFloat($('#farmer').css('width'));

        var sandwichX = parseFloat($('#sandwich').css('marginLeft'));
        var sandwichY = parseFloat($('#sandwich').css('marginTop'));
        var sandwichHeight = parseFloat($('#sandwich').css('height'));
        var sandwichWidth = parseFloat($('#sandwich').css('width'));

    }, 10)

}
```

7. Every ten milliseconds, we get the height, width, X, and Y values for the farmer and the sandwich. Remember the really mathematical part earlier that **tells the page when two items are touching**? We need to create another one!

```javascript
if (sandwichX > leftBuffer && sandwichX < rightBuffer && (sandwichY+sandwichHeight) > farmerY && sandwichY < downBuffer){

    $('#sandwich').remove();
    score = score+50;
}
```

8. Now we need to **add *sandwichContact()* to our *startGame* function.** We've added a lot of features to our game since we started. By now, it should look like this:

```
function startGame(){

    score = 0;

    $('#gamearea').append("<img id = 'farmer' src = 'assets/farmer.jpg' />")

    createPig()
    getContact()
    timer();
    createSandwich();
    sandwichContact();

}
```

9. **Save everything, and try playing your game.** How is it? Is everything working like you expected?

Remember: you're the boss! If there's something you don't like, you can always change it.

For instance, it's pretty tough to reach the sandwiches in time, isn't it? There are two ways of tweaking this: changing the farmer's speed, or changing how often sandwiches appear. If the pigs are annoying you, feel free to change how often they appear.

SOME FINAL CHALLENGES   X

The following tasks will check to see if you've understood all that we've covered so far! Everything you need to complete them is mentioned somewhere in this book. If you're stuck, try looking back over earlier chapters. You can do it!

- Change the background image.

- Make the farmer smaller.

- Make sandwiches bounce when touched.

- Make a sound play when you pick up a sandwich.

- Create a popup when the game ends.

- Draw a chicken and have it run across the screen when the user clicks.

<MISSION COMPLETED>

A NOTE TO THE READER

If you've made it this far, congratulations! Some of the things we've covered have been pretty tricky to understand, but coding is just like painting or playing sports—the more you do it, the better you get.

The good news is that we've only covered coding for the web. There are all kinds of coding languages out there, each with its own strengths and weaknesses. Some, such as Java, are used to make apps for your cell phone, while others (such as Python) aren't as fancy, but are great for science.

By following along with this book, you've taken your first steps on the journey to being an incredible coder. It's going to be a long road, and sometimes you won't know how to solve a problem, but keep on trying—you'll feel amazing when you find the answer.

GLOSSARY

Don't know what a particular word means? I've made a list of all the words you might be confused about and explained them right here. Check it out, and impress your friends!

Array: A special variable that holds multiple values instead of just one.

Assets: Things such as images and audio files that are used with your website or program.

CSS: Cascading Style Sheets. We use CSS to change the way elements on an HTML page look or act.

Element: An item on a web page. An element can be anything: an image, a <div>, a table, even text.

Function: A collection of code that is grouped together so it can be run at a specific time, without having to type it out multiple times.

HTML: HyperText Markup Language. This language is used to create the basic structure of a website.

JavaScript: A scripting language that is used to add extra features or functionality to a website.

jQuery: A JavaScript plugin that can change the way users interact with elements on a web page.

Loop: A way of running a section of code multiple times in a row without typing it all out each time.

Parameter: A value that is passed to a function, changing its results.

Pixel: One of the tiny dots that your screen uses to display content.

Plugin: A package of code designed to improve existing software. These often add new features, or make it easier to do complicated things.

Scratch: A website that lets you build basic programs using blocks instead of typing code.

setInterval: A JavaScript function that lets you repeatedly run a section of code at a specific time.

Sprite: An image used as part of a game. Only things that can be interacted with are sprites—for instance, a background image isn't a sprite, but the main character image is.

Tag: The building blocks used in HTML websites. Tags are always surrounded with pointy brackets, and usually close with another set and a forward slash in front of the first letter. For instance: <head> opens the tag and </head> closes it.

Variable: A value that is given a name and stored to be used again later.

<NEED SOME HELP?>

TROUBLESHOOTING

If your code isn't working properly, don't worry! Nobody makes programs that run perfectly the first time they try. In fact, facing problems will actually make you a better coder as you figure out where you went wrong. Below, I've listed some common coding problems and their solutions.

Text is showing up on my web page when it shouldn't be

Usually, this means you haven't closed an HTML tag properly. For instance, if you've typed <p> </> instead of <p></p>, your web page will say "</>".

It could also be that you haven't closed your quotation marks properly. If you have quotation marks inside another set, it's important to use both single marks ('test') and double marks ("test") to help keep things easy to understand.

This would work:

```
$('#mainsection').append("<img class = 'egg'/>");
```

This would not:

```
$('#mainsection').append("<img class = "egg"/>");
```

In the second image, jQuery thinks we've tried to connect a string saying "<img class =" to the word "egg". Instead, "egg" should be in single quotation marks.

A JavaScript function doesn't run

There are a lot of possible reasons why nothing happens when your function is supposed to run. However, most web browsers have an easy way to find out what the issue is. If you press the F12 key on your keyboard and click the "Console" tab that appears on the right-hand side, you'll see some red text explaining what the problem is.

```
⊗ Uncaught SyntaxError:          animation.html:59
  Unexpected token )
```

Here, it tells us that the problem is in the "animation.html" page, near line 59. Now, the problem is that we've forgotten to close a bracket, so we'll need to find the missing one and enter it in the right place.

Another common issue is typing a variable name incorrectly. In the case below, the variable is actually called *eggCount*, not *egCount*. Simply type the correct name and the code will run.

```
⊗ ▶Uncaught ReferenceError: egCount is not defined   animation.html:67
```

Here are a few things to do if you really can't find the problem:

- Make sure all of your functions and variables are typed correctly.

- If your jQuery isn't working, make sure you've added the links to the <head> section of your HTML page.

- Check your setInterval functions. If the repetition time is set too high, it might seem like nothing is happening.

Your CSS isn't working

The most common reason for CSS not applying is forgetting to add the link to the top of your HTML page. It could also be that you've mistyped something, such as "bacground-color" instead of "background-color".

If you've checked both of these things, make sure you're actually pointing to the right CSS file. The name of the CSS file should go into the "href" part of this code:

```
<link rel="stylesheet" type="text/css" href="style.css">
```

Having problems with a specific element? Remember that to select an object by its ID, you have to add a "#" in front. To select one based on its class, you add a dot (.):

```
#creeper{

    max-width:8%;

}

.defeated{

    -webkit-animation: spin 0.1s 3;

}
```

Images are too big, too small, or partly off the screen

Computer monitors come in all shapes and sizes. All of the sizes given in this book are fine when viewed on a 24-inch screen at 1920x1080p resolution. That said, if you find that some things look strange, feel free to change their sizes in the CSS file. There's no problem with this at all! It won't change the way your code runs, although you may have to adjust the sizes of some other elements as well, particularly for the animation chapter.

Only some of the code works

All of the code in this book was tested in Google Chrome (Version 65.0.3325.181). Unfortunately, not all web browsers have the same HTML5 compatibility, which means certain parts might not work correctly in other browsers.

If you're experiencing issues while using Google Chrome, turn off any popup blockers or ad-blocking extensions you might have. You can always reactivate these when you're finished working through the activities.